BOR~ ____ ~

TRAVEL GUIDE

2024

The Ultimate Guide And Tips On Where To stay, What To Do, What To Eat In Bora Bora And A Lot More

Ruest Lizotte

Pearl of the Pacific

Nestled in the heart of the South Pacific Ocean, Bora Bora is a name that conjures images of pristine beaches, crystal-clear waters, and overwater bungalows. This small island, part of the French Polynesia archipelago, is often referred to as the "Pearl of the Pacific" and is renowned for its breathtaking natural beauty. With its stunning landscapes, rich culture, and luxurious resorts, Bora Bora is a destination that captivates the hearts and imaginations of travelers from all corners of the globe.

At the geographical coordinates of 16.5 degrees south latitude and 151.75 degrees west longitude, Bora Bora is located about 230 kilometers (143 miles) northwest of Tahiti, the largest island in French Polynesia. Its remote location in the middle of the Pacific Ocean ensures that Bora Bora remains relatively untouched and maintains its unspoiled charm.

One of the most iconic features of Bora Bora is its strikingly beautiful lagoon, which is surrounded by a barrier reef. The lagoon is home to an astonishing array of marine life, including colorful coral reefs, tropical fish, and even sharks and rays.

Above the tranquil waters of the lagoon, Bora Bora's world-famous overwater bungalows offer a unique and romantic accommodation experience. These bungalows perched on stilts allow guests to wake up to the gentle lapping of the waves beneath them, with stunning views of the lagoon and Mount Otemanu, the island's highest peak.

The island's dramatic landscapes are dominated by Mount Otemanu, a dormant volcano that rises 2,385 feet (727 meters) above sea level. This majestic peak is the centerpiece of Bora Bora's skyline and offers hikers a challenging yet rewarding trek, with panoramic views of the island and its surroundings. For those seeking less strenuous adventures, there are numerous opportunities for off-road tours and guided hikes through lush forests and secluded beaches.

Bora Bora's culture is deeply rooted in Polynesian traditions and hospitality. The Tahitian people, known for their warm and welcoming nature, provide visitors with an authentic and memorable experience. Traditional dance and music performances, as well as local crafts, are showcased in cultural exhibitions, allowing tourists to immerse themselves in the island's heritage.

Bora Bora is a true paradise on Earth, offering unparalleled natural beauty, vibrant culture, and numerous activities for all types of travelers.

Excellent Reasons to Visit Bora Bora

Stunning Overwater Bungalows: Bora Bora is famous for its luxurious overwater bungalows. These enchanting accommodations, perched above the crystal-clear waters, offer a unique and romantic experience. Imagine waking up to the gentle lapping of the waves beneath you and having direct access to the lagoon for a morning swim. Bora Bora is the epitome of tropical opulence, with resorts like the St. Regis and Four Seasons offering some of the most exquisite overwater bungalows in the world.

Turquoise Waters and Coral Reefs: The island's lagoon is a mesmerizing shade of turquoise, encircled by a protective barrier reef. Snorkeling and scuba diving enthusiasts will find a vibrant underwater world teeming with colorful coral reefs, tropical fish, and other marine life. You can also take a boat tour to explore the diverse coral gardens and swim with graceful rays and sharks, offering an unforgettable underwater adventure.

Pristine Beaches: Bora Bora boasts some of the most picturesque beaches in the world. Bora Bora beaches are renowned for their powdery white sand and crystal-clear waters. Relax under swaying palm trees, swim in the calm lagoon, or simply take in the stunning views.

The island's beaches provide an idyllic setting for unwinding and soaking up the sun.

Polynesian Culture: Bora Bora's rich Polynesian heritage is a treasure to explore. The local Tahitian people are known for their warmth and hospitality. Engage with the culture through traditional dance and music performances, art exhibitions, and workshops. Learn about the significance of the tiare flower and the art of pareo tying, and leave with a deeper understanding of the island's traditions.

Delicious Cuisine: Tahitian cuisine is a delightful blend of fresh, local ingredients. Seafood takes center stage, with dishes like poisson cru, a marinated raw fish salad, being a local favorite. You can also enjoy delicious coconut-based dishes and an abundance of tropical fruits. Dining on the beach or at the island's upscale restaurants adds a special touch to the culinary experience.

Adventure and Watersports: Bora Bora offers an array of thrilling activities for adventure seekers. Jet skiing, paddleboarding, and kite surfing are just a few of the options available. Explore the island's rugged interior on an off-road safari, discovering hidden waterfalls and lush landscapes. For those with a penchant for water-based adventures, the lagoon is perfect for kayaking, parasailing, and wakeboarding.

Wellness and Relaxation: Bora Bora is not only a destination for the adventurous but also for those seeking relaxation. World-class spas and wellness centers provide an array of rejuvenating treatments, massages, and beauty therapies. What better way to unwind than with a spa session while surrounded by the beauty of paradise?

Family-Friendly Environment: While Bora Bora is renowned for its romantic getaways and honeymoon retreats, it's also a family-friendly destination. Many resorts offer kid's clubs, making it suitable for family vacations. Children can enjoy beachside activities and explore the island's natural wonders.

Diverse Accommodation Options: Bora Bora caters to a wide range of budgets and preferences. While it's famous for its luxury resorts and overwater bungalows, there are more budget-friendly options, including cozy guesthouses and lodges. Regardless of your choice, the island's enchanting beauty remains accessible to all.

Bora Bora is a destination that offers a perfect blend of natural beauty, adventure, relaxation, and cultural immersion. Its allure extends to a wide range of travelers, from honeymooners to families, and solo adventurers.

Chapter 1

Top Attractions

Here are the top attractions that make Bora Bora a paradise like no other.

Average fee price range (USD)

Matira Beach: This pristine stretch of powdery white sand is one of the most famous beaches on the island. Matira Beach is perfect for swimming, sunbathing, and enjoying the tranquil waters of the lagoon.

Price range: Free

Mount Otemanu: This dormant volcano, towering at 2,385 feet (727 meters), dominates the island's landscape. For the adventurous, hiking to its summit offers panoramic views that are truly breathtaking.

Price range: $50-$100 per person for a guided hike

Overwater Bungalows: Bora Bora is renowned for its luxurious overwater bungalows, which provide a unique and romantic accommodation experience. Staying in one of these iconic bungalows is a must for many visitors.

Price range: $500-$1000 per night

Coral Gardens: The island's lagoon is home to a dazzling underwater world, with colorful coral reefs and an abundance of marine life. Snorkeling and scuba diving are popular activities to explore these mesmerizing coral gardens.

Price range: $50-$100 per person for a snorkeling or diving tour

Shark and Ray Feeding: Take a guided boat tour to swim with and feed black-tip reef sharks and stingrays. This unforgettable experience allows you to get up close and personal with these majestic creatures.

Price range: $100-$150 per person

Polynesian Culture: Bora Bora's rich Polynesian heritage is a treasure to discover. Engage with the local culture through traditional dance and music performances, art exhibitions, and cultural workshops.

Price range: $50-$100 per person for a cultural show and dinner

Bora Bora Lagoonarium: This unique attraction is a natural aquarium where you can snorkel and observe a wide variety of fish and marine species in their natural habitat. It's an educational and fascinating experience for all ages.

Price range: $50-$100 per person for a day pass

Matira Point: This scenic lookout offers breathtaking views of Matira Beach, the lagoon, and the surrounding islands. It's a popular spot for sunset photography.

Price range: Free

Marae Temples: These ancient Polynesian temples are scattered throughout the island. They offer insight into Bora Bora's historical and cultural significance. The most well-preserved marae is at Fare Opu.

Price range: Free

Faanui Bay: This charming village on the northwest coast of the island provides a glimpse into local life. Stroll through the streets, visit the small church, and interact with the friendly residents.

Price range: Free

Leopard Rays Trench: This snorkeling site is known for its remarkable abundance of graceful spotted eagle rays. It's a must-visit for underwater enthusiasts looking to witness these beautiful creatures in their natural habitat.

Price range: $50-$100

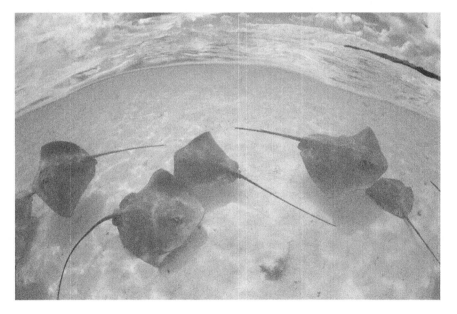

Bloody Mary's Restaurant: A famous eatery on the island, Bloody Mary's is known for its fresh seafood and rustic atmosphere. Dine beneath the thatched roof and enjoy the charm of this iconic establishment.

Price range: $25-$50

Bora Bora Turtle Center: This conservation center is dedicated to the protection and rehabilitation of sea turtles. It offers an educational experience where you can learn about these incredible creatures and their conservation.

Price range: $20-$30

Art Galleries: The island boasts several art galleries showcasing the work of local artists. These galleries offer a chance to explore the vibrant art scene of Bora Bora.

Price range: Free, but prices vary for purchases

Fauna and Flora: Bora Bora's lush landscapes and botanical gardens are home to a wide variety of plant and animal species. Take a guided tour to learn about the island's unique ecology.

Price range: Free to explore on your own, but prices vary for guided tours

Sunset Cruises: End your day with a romantic sunset cruise around the lagoon. Enjoy a glass of champagne as you watch the sun dip below the horizon, casting a warm and colorful glow over the island.

Price range: $50-$100

These top attractions in Bora Bora are just a glimpse of what this remarkable island has to offer, making it a truly extraordinary destination in the South Pacific.

Best festivals

While Bora Bora may not host as many festivals as some larger destinations, it does have a few annual events that offer visitors a unique glimpse into the local culture and traditions. Here are some of the best festivals in Bora Bora.

1. **Heiva i Bora Bora** (July): Heiva is a significant festival celebrated throughout French Polynesia, and Bora Bora participates with enthusiasm. This event typically takes place in July and includes a wide range of cultural and artistic performances. It's a time when locals showcase their traditional dance, music, and crafts. The festival often features vibrant parades, sporting events, and traditional ceremonies.

2. **Taurua Nui Bora Bora Canoe Race** (June or July): This exciting outrigger canoe race is a major sporting event in Bora Bora. Canoe teams from different islands in French Polynesia gather to compete in various categories. The races are held in June or July and offer a unique opportunity to witness the strength and skill of local athletes.

3. **Independence Day** (July 14th): While this is not a festival in the traditional sense, Bastille Day is celebrated with enthusiasm in Bora Bora. The local communities often organize parades, fireworks, and

other patriotic events to mark France's national holiday on July 14th. It's a great time to experience the fusion of French and Polynesian cultures on the island.

4. **Heiva Hura i Bora Bora** (September): Heiva Hura, also known as the Bora Bora Dance Festival, is an exciting event that celebrates Polynesian dance. Dance troupes from all over Bora Bora and French Polynesia gather to compete in various dance categories, showcasing traditional and contemporary choreography. This festival is an excellent opportunity to immerse yourself in the vibrant world of Tahitian dance.

5. **Maupiti Heiva** (July): While not on Bora Bora, the Maupiti Heiva is an event in a nearby island, Maupiti. It's worth mentioning because it's a short boat ride away from Bora Bora, and if you happen to visit during July, you can easily attend. This celebration features traditional Polynesian dance performances, sporting events, and cultural exhibitions.

6. **St. Regis Bora Bora's Bora Bora Gourmet Festival** (June): Though not a traditional Polynesian festival, this culinary event is a must for food enthusiasts. The St. Regis Bora Bora Resort hosts the Bora Bora Gourmet Festival in June, featuring internationally renowned chefs who create exquisite dishes with

local ingredients. It's a gastronomic journey that showcases the fusion of French and Polynesian cuisines.

7. **Bora Bora Liquid Festival** (Dates Vary): While the Bora Bora Liquid Festival does not have fixed annual dates, it's an event that caters to watersports enthusiasts. This multi-day festival typically includes activities such as paddleboarding, windsurfing, and kiteboarding competitions, making it an exciting event for those who want to explore Bora Bora's aquatic adventures.

8. **Annual Bora Bora Half Marathon** (June): For those with a passion for running, the Bora Bora Half Marathon is a unique way to explore the island. Held in June, the event features races of various distances, including a half marathon, 10K, and 5K. Participants get to enjoy stunning scenery while taking part in this athletic challenge.

Bora Bora's festivals offer an authentic and intimate look into the island's culture and traditions.

Best museums

Bora Bora have a few small museums and cultural centers that offer insights into its history, culture, and natural heritage. Here, we'll explore some of the best museums and cultural sites on the island.

1. **Marae Temples**: Marae temples are sacred Polynesian sites that hold cultural and historical significance. Bora Bora has a few of these archaeological sites, where visitors can explore ancient stone structures and learn about the island's early history and religious practices. Maraes like Marae Fare Opu and Marae Anini are good places to start.

2. **Art Galleries**: Bora Bora is home to a handful of art galleries that showcase the work of local and Polynesian artists. These galleries feature a range of art, including traditional paintings, sculptures, and crafts. It's an opportunity to explore the vibrant art scene of Bora Bora and perhaps purchase a unique piece of local art as a memento.

3. **Pearl Farms**: Although not traditional museums, the pearl farms in Bora Bora offer fascinating insights into the pearl cultivation process. Visitors can take guided tours to learn about the delicate art of pearl farming, from the seeding of oysters to the harvesting of

exquisite black pearls. These tours provide a deeper appreciation for this iconic Polynesian industry.

4. **Coral World**: Coral World is an interactive and educational marine experience where visitors can explore various marine life and interact with sea creatures like turtles and rays. While it's not a museum in the conventional sense, it offers a chance to learn about the marine biodiversity and conservation efforts in the area.

5. **St. James Place and Museum**: This small museum is dedicated to the history of the island and provides a glimpse into the culture and traditions of the Polynesian people. It offers valuable insights into Bora Bora's past.

6. **House of Love**: The House of Love is an artisanal center and a place to explore traditional Polynesian crafts. Visitors can watch local artisans at work, creating intricate jewelry, carvings, and other handmade items. This center provides an opportunity to learn about the craftsmanship that plays a vital role in Polynesian culture.

7. **Cultural Workshops**: While not traditional museums, some resorts on Bora Bora offer cultural workshops where guests can learn about Polynesian traditions, crafts, and dance. These workshops provide a hands-

on experience and an opportunity to immerse yourself in the local culture.

8. **Bora Bora Original Coconut Creations**: This charming shop and workshop offer visitors a chance to witness the traditional art of crafting items from coconuts. The skilled artisans demonstrate the process of turning coconuts into unique souvenirs and functional items.

Chapter 2

Planning your trip

Visa and passport requirements

It is essential to understand the visa and passport requirements when planning a trip to Bora Bora. Below we will explore the visa and passport requirements specific to Bora Bora, including who needs a visa, visa types and the application process.

Passport Requirements for Bora Bora

Before delving into visa requirements, it's crucial to understand the passport requirements for traveling to Bora Bora:

Passport Validity

To enter Bora Bora, travelers must possess a valid passport. The passport must be valid for at least six months beyond the intended date of departure from Bora Bora. It's essential to ensure that your passport meets this validity requirement before embarking on your journey.

Blank Passport Pages

Most countries, including Bora Bora, require that your passport has at least one or two blank visa pages. These pages are crucial for visa stamps and entry/exit records. Ensure that your passport has enough available pages to accommodate these requirements.

Passport Expiration Date

While the passport validity of six months beyond your departure date is a standard requirement, it's advisable to renew your passport well in advance of your trip if it's close to the expiration date. Some countries may require a passport to be valid for even longer than six months beyond the departure date.

Visa Requirements for Bora Bora

While many travelers can visit Bora Bora for tourism without a visa, it's essential to understand that these regulations can change. Therefore, it's advisable to confirm the most up-to-date information from your local embassy or consulate before planning your trip.

Visa-Free Travel for Short-Term Tourism

For short-term tourism visits (usually up to 90 days), citizens of many countries, including the United States, Canada, the European Union member states, and many others, do not require a visa to enter Bora Bora.

Travelers from these countries can typically enter Bora Bora for leisure purposes with just a valid passport. It's essential to check with your local embassy or consulate to verify if you are eligible for visa-free travel.

Visa on Arrival

In some cases, travelers who are not eligible for visa-free travel to Bora Bora can obtain a visa upon arrival at the airport. These visas are often granted for short visits and tourism purposes. The process usually involves filling out an application form and paying a fee upon arrival. The length of stay permitted with a visa on arrival can vary, so it's important to check the specific regulations for your nationality.

Visa Requirements for Extended Stays or Other Purposes

If you plan to stay in Bora Bora for purposes other than tourism, such as work or long-term residence, you will likely need to obtain the appropriate visa before your arrival. These visas are subject to specific requirements and application processes. It's essential to consult the Bora Bora embassy or consulate in your home country for detailed information regarding the specific visa type you require and the application process.

Valid Travel Documents

It's crucial to have all your travel documents in order before boarding your flight to Bora Bora. This includes your passport, any required visa, return or onward ticket, and any other documents requested by the Bora Bora immigration authorities.

Special Visa and Entry Requirements

Travelers with special circumstances, such as those with dual citizenship or travelers with criminal records, should seek guidance from the relevant authorities well in advance of their trip. It's essential to understand any unique visa or entry requirements that may apply to your situation.

Tips for a Smooth Journey to Bora Bora

To ensure a hassle-free and enjoyable trip to Bora Bora, consider the following tips:

Apply for a Visa in Advance: If your trip involves purposes other than short-term tourism, such as work or long-term residence, apply for the necessary visa well in advance of your travel date.

Gather Required Documents: Collect all the necessary documents, including your passport, visa, return or onward ticket, and any other documents required for entry into Bora Bora.

Travel Insurance: Consider obtaining comprehensive travel insurance to protect yourself in case of unexpected events or emergencies during your trip.

Local Embassy or Consulate: Keep the contact information for the Bora Bora embassy or consulate in your home country. They can provide essential information and assistance if you encounter any issues during your trip.

Local Laws and Regulations: Familiarize yourself with the local laws and regulations in Bora Bora. Adhering to the country's rules and customs will ensure a respectful and trouble-free visit.

Travel Documentation Copies: Make copies of your passport, visa, and other essential travel documents. Store these copies separately from the originals to have a backup in case of loss or theft.

In conclusion, the visa and passport requirements for Bora Bora are generally straightforward for short-term tourists from many countries.

Best time to visit Bora Bora

Choosing the best time to visit depends on your preferences and what you want to experience on the island. Here's a breakdown of the different seasons and what you can expect during each:

1. **Dry Season (May to October):**

- **Best for**: Ideal weather, outdoor activities, and less rainfall.

- **Weather**: Bora Bora's dry season runs from May to October. During this period, the weather is generally pleasant and dry, with lower humidity. You can expect plenty of sunshine and cooler temperatures compared to the wet season.

- **Outdoor Activities**: The dry season is the best time for outdoor activities such as snorkeling, scuba diving, water sports, and hiking. The clear skies and calm seas make it perfect for exploring the underwater world and enjoying the beaches.

2. **Wet Season (November to April):**

- **Best for**: Fewer tourists and budget-conscious travelers.

- **Weather**: The wet season in Bora Bora typically occurs from November to April. This period experiences more rain and higher humidity. Showers and occasional tropical storms are more likely during these months.

- **Fewer Crowds**: One advantage of visiting during the wet season is that there are fewer tourists, which can make for a more peaceful and intimate experience on the island.

- **Budget Travel**: Accommodation and activity prices may be lower during the wet season, making it a more budget-friendly option for travelers.

3. **High Season (June to August):**

Best for: Ideal weather and honeymooners.

Weather: June to August falls within the dry season and is considered high season in Bora Bora. The weather during this time is usually perfect, with lots of sunshine, warm temperatures, and clear skies.

Honeymooners: Many couples choose to visit Bora Bora during the high season, making it a popular destination for honeymooners. It's an ideal time for a romantic getaway.

4. **Whale Watching (July to October):**

Best for: Whale watching enthusiasts.

Weather: From July to October, you have an excellent chance to witness humpback whales in the waters around Bora Bora. These majestic creatures come to the area to give birth and nurse their calves.

- **Whale Tours**: Numerous tour operators offer whale-watching excursions during this time, providing an opportunity to see these magnificent animals up close.

5. **Tahiti's Heiva Festival (July):**

- **Best for**: Cultural enthusiasts.

- **Festival**: Bora Bora is part of French Polynesia, and in July, you can experience the vibrant Heiva Festival.

The best time to visit Bora Bora depends on your preferences and what you want to experience during your trip. The dry season, from May to October, is generally the most popular time for travelers due to ideal weather conditions. However, visiting during the wet season or off-peak months can offer unique advantages, such as fewer crowds and budget-friendly options.

Transportation options to Bora Bora

Transportation Options to Bora Bora: Navigating Paradise

Let's explore the various transportation options available to reach and navigate this idyllic paradise, including air travel, boat transfers and tips to make your journey smooth and enjoyable.

Getting to Bora Bora

Flights to Bora Bora

Most travelers to Bora Bora arrive via air travel. The primary gateway to the island is Bora Bora Airport (IATA: BOB), which is officially known as Motu Mute Airport. Here are the key aspects of reaching Bora Bora by air:

International Flights:

- **Papeete, Tahiti (PPT)**: Most international travelers first arrive in Tahiti, French Polynesia's capital. Faa'a International Airport in Tahiti (Papeete) is the main entry point for international flights. From there, you can connect to a domestic flight to Bora Bora.

- **Los Angeles (LAX)**: Some travelers coming from the United States may find direct flights from Los Angeles to Bora Bora Airport (BOB) through Air Tahiti or other carriers. These flights typically stop in Tahiti for a layover.

- **Other International Gateways**: Depending on your location, you might connect through other international airports before reaching Tahiti and then Bora Bora.

Domestic Flights:

- **Air Tahiti**: Air Tahiti is the primary domestic airline in French Polynesia. They operate regular flights between Tahiti (Papeete) and Bora Bora Airport. Flight durations from Tahiti to Bora Bora are relatively short, typically around 45 minutes.

Transfers from Bora Bora Airport to Your Accommodation

Once you arrive at Bora Bora Airport (BOB), you'll need to transfer to your accommodation. The primary mode of transportation for this leg of your journey is typically by boat. Many Bora Bora resorts provide complimentary boat transfers for their guests from the airport to their overwater bungalows or beachfront villas.

If your accommodation does not offer complimentary transfers, you can arrange for a private boat transfer in advance. It's essential to confirm your transfer details with your accommodation when booking your stay.

Getting Around Bora Bora

Boat Transfers and Water Taxis

Bora Bora is renowned for its stunning lagoon and water-based activities. As a result, boat transportation plays a significant role in navigating the island. Here's what you need to know:

- **Boat Shuttles**: Most resorts and accommodations in Bora Bora provide boat shuttles for guests. These shuttles transport visitors between their accommodations, the main island, and the airport. They are often included in the cost of your stay.

- **Water Taxis**: Water taxis are readily available on Bora Bora and offer a convenient way to explore the island. You can hire water taxis for point-to-point transportation between various locations, such as restaurants, shops, and popular attractions.

- **Lagoon Tours**: Bora Bora is famous for its lagoon tours. These excursions typically include boat transportation and allow you to explore the coral gardens, snorkel, swim with sharks and rays, and enjoy the beauty of the island's surroundings.

Bicycles and Scooters

While boats are the primary mode of transportation on the water, bicycles and scooters are popular choices for getting around the main island. Here's what you need to know:

- **Bicycles**: Many accommodations provide bicycles for their guests, allowing them to explore the island at their own pace. Bora Bora's flat terrain makes cycling a practical and enjoyable option.

- **Scooters**: Scooter rentals are available on the main island. Renting a scooter can be a fun and efficient way to see the sights, visit local restaurants, and experience the island's natural beauty.

Four-Wheel Drive and Guided Tours

If you prefer to explore Bora Bora's interior and more remote locations, guided tours and four-wheel drive excursions are excellent choices. Here's what you need to know:

- **Guided Tours**: Various tour operators offer guided excursions that allow you to explore the island's lush landscapes, visit World War II remnants, and learn about the local culture. These tours often include transportation to and from your accommodation.

- **Four-Wheel Drive Rentals**: Renting a four-wheel drive vehicle is another way to explore the island's interior and reach viewpoints that offer breathtaking panoramas of the lagoon and Mount Otemanu. Keep in mind that driving is on the right side of the road.

Tips for a Smooth Journey in Bora Bora

To ensure a smooth and enjoyable journey to and around Bora Bora, consider the following tips:

Book Transfers in Advance

If your accommodation does not provide complimentary transfers from Bora Bora Airport, it's advisable to book your transfer in advance to avoid any hassles upon arrival. There are reliable transfer providers that can ensure you reach your destination seamlessly.

Confirm Transportation Details

Whether you're relying on your accommodation's boat shuttle or water taxis, it's crucial to confirm your transportation details and schedules in advance to ensure a stress-free experience.

Respect Local Transportation Guidelines

When using local transportation, such as bicycles and scooters, adhere to local traffic rules and regulations. Ensure that you have the necessary licenses and permits, and always wear helmets when riding scooters.

Tour Operator Reputability

When booking guided tours or four-wheel drive excursions, choose tour operators with a good reputation and positive reviews. These operators are more likely to provide an enjoyable and safe experience.

Water Safety

When participating in water-based activities or lagoon tours, prioritize safety. Always follow the guidance of your tour operator and use the provided safety equipment, especially when snorkeling or swimming with marine life.

Preserve the Environment

Bora Bora is known for its pristine natural beauty. Do your part in preserving the environment by not disturbing marine life, disposing of waste responsibly, and participating in conservation efforts when possible.

Language and Currency

While French is the official language of Bora Bora, many locals also speak Tahitian, and English is commonly used in the tourism industry. It's helpful to have a basic understanding of these languages. Additionally, the currency in Bora Bora is the French Pacific Franc (XPF).

In conclusion, transportation to and around Bora Bora is an essential aspect of planning your visit to this paradise. By understanding the options available, booking transfers in advance, and respecting local guidelines, you can ensure a seamless and enjoyable journey in this idyllic destination.

Getting Around Bora Bora

Getting Around Bora Bora: Navigating Paradise with Ease

Getting around this small island is relatively straightforward, as it offers various transportation options to explore its stunning landscapes and enjoy its breathtaking lagoon. Below we will delve into the different ways of getting around Bora Bora, from land to sea, while highlighting key transportation methods and tips for a seamless and memorable visit.

Land Transportation

Bicycles

Bicycles are a popular mode of land transportation on Bora Bora. They offer a fantastic way to explore the main island and take in the scenic views at a leisurely pace. Here's what you need to know about cycling on the island:

- **Bicycle Rentals**: Many accommodations, especially guesthouses and smaller hotels, provide complimentary bicycles for their guests to use during their stay. If your accommodation doesn't offer this service, there are local rental shops where you can rent bicycles for a reasonable fee.

- **Terrain**: Bora Bora is relatively flat, making it an ideal location for cycling. Most of the island's roads are in good condition, and you can easily explore both the coastal areas and the interior. Keep in mind that some roads might be a bit hilly, so choose your routes accordingly.

- **Safety**: When cycling in Bora Bora, always prioritize safety. Wear a helmet, use lights when riding at night, and obey local traffic laws. Roads can be narrow, so be cautious and respectful of other road users.

Scooters

Scooters are another option for land transportation on Bora Bora. They offer a bit more speed and flexibility compared to bicycles. Here's what you should know:

- **Scooter Rentals**: You can rent scooters from various rental companies on the island. It's essential to have a valid driver's license, and you may need an international driving permit depending on your home country.

- **Road Conditions**: Most of the main roads on Bora Bora are in good condition and suitable for scooters. However, some roads can be narrow, so exercise caution. It's also important to drive on the right side of the road.

- **Exploration**: Scooters are a convenient way to explore the island's interior and visit points of interest such as local shops, restaurants, and viewpoints offering stunning vistas of the lagoon and Mount Otemanu.

Four-Wheel Drive Vehicles

Four-wheel drive vehicles are ideal for exploring Bora Bora's rugged interior, especially if you want to reach some of the more remote viewpoints and historical sites. Here's what you need to know about using four-wheel drive vehicles:

- **Rentals**: You can rent four-wheel drive vehicles from local car rental agencies. These vehicles are equipped to handle the sometimes-challenging terrain in the island's interior.

- **Tours**: If you prefer not to drive yourself, you can join guided four-wheel drive tours. These tours often include knowledgeable guides who provide insights into the island's history, culture, and natural beauty.

- **Off-Roading**: Exploring Bora Bora's interior by four-wheel drive allows you to access secluded beaches, World War II relics, and panoramic viewpoints. Keep in mind that some roads may be unpaved, so an off-road vehicle is ideal for such exploration.

Water Transportation

Boat Shuttles

Given Bora Bora's geography, **boat shuttles** are a primary mode of water transportation on the island. They offer convenient and efficient ways to move between accommodations, the main island, and the airport. Here's what you should know:

- **Resort Services**: Most of the luxury resorts in Bora Bora provide complimentary boat transfers for their guests. These shuttles pick up guests from Bora Bora Airport and transport them to their accommodations. Additionally, they offer regular boat services to the main island.

- **Water Taxi Services**: Water taxis are readily available on the island and offer on-demand or scheduled transfers. They can take you between various locations, including restaurants, shops, and popular attractions.

- **Excursions**: Many lagoon excursions and tours are conducted using boats, making them a great way to explore the beautiful waters of Bora Bora. These tours often include opportunities for snorkeling, swimming with marine life, and picnicking on motus (small islets).

Kayaking and Paddleboarding

Kayaking and paddleboarding are excellent ways to explore Bora Bora's tranquil lagoon at your own pace. Here's what you need to know about these water-based activities:

- **Rental Availability**: Many accommodations offer kayaks and paddleboards for their guests. It's a delightful way to take in the natural surroundings and enjoy some exercise while exploring the lagoon.

- **Safety**: When kayaking or paddleboarding, ensure you have the necessary safety equipment, such as life vests. The lagoon is known for its calm and clear waters, making it perfect for these activities.

In conclusion, getting around Bora Bora is an integral part of experiencing the island's natural beauty and local culture.

Budget

Bora Bora is a stunning and luxurious destination, but it's essential to be aware of the budget you'll need for your trip. Here's some information on Bora Bora's budget:

Budget: Bora Bora is known for its luxury and exclusivity, and as such, it can be a relatively expensive destination. The cost of your trip will depend on various factors, including your choice of accommodation, dining preferences, and the activities you wish to pursue. Here's a rough breakdown of budget categories:

1. **Accommodation:** The bulk of your expenses may come from your choice of accommodation. Overwater bungalows and luxury resorts can be quite expensive, with nightly rates ranging from $500 to well over $1,000 or more.

2. **Dining:** Dining in Bora Bora can also be costly, particularly in upscale restaurants. A three-course meal for two in a mid-range restaurant can cost around $100 to $200. To save money, consider eating at local snack bars and small eateries, where prices are more budget-friendly.

3. **Activities:** Excursions and water-based activities, such as snorkeling, diving, and jet skiing, can add to your expenses. The prices for these activities vary,

but you can expect to pay a few hundred dollars for some of the more exclusive experiences.

4. **Transportation:** Depending on where you're traveling from, flights to Bora Bora can be a significant expense. Once on the island, getting around by boat or land will require additional transportation costs.

5. **Miscellaneous:** Souvenirs, drinks, and other incidentals will also contribute to your overall expenses.

To make your Bora Bora trip more budget-friendly, consider the following tips:

- Look for package deals or all-inclusive resort options that can help you save on meals and activities.

- Visit local markets and food trucks for more affordable dining options.

- Prioritize the activities that matter most to you and focus on those to control costs.

- Plan your trip during the shoulder season, which can offer more competitive prices for accommodations and activities.

It's important to set a realistic budget for your Bora Bora trip, taking into account your preferences and financial capacity. Bora Bora offers a range of experiences, and with careful planning, you can enjoy this paradise without breaking the bank.

Chapter 3

Bora Bora travel essentials

When planning a trip to Bora Bora, it's essential to pack wisely and prepare for the unique experiences this destination offers. Here are the travel essentials you should consider for your Bora Bora adventure:

1. **Travel Insurance**:

- Consider purchasing comprehensive travel insurance that covers trip cancellations, medical emergencies, and travel-related mishaps. Verify that your insurance includes activities like water sports and lagoon excursions.

2. **Local Currency and Credit Cards**:

- The currency used in French Polynesia is the French Pacific Franc (XPF). While credit cards are widely accepted in hotels and upscale restaurants, it's a good idea to carry some XPF for small purchases, tips, and local markets.

3. **Power Adapters**:

- French Polynesia uses European-style power outlets with a standard voltage of 220V. Make sure to pack power adapters or voltage converters if necessary.

4. **Health and Medications**:

- Bring any prescription medications you require and carry them in their original containers. It's a good idea to pack a basic travel medical kit with essentials like pain relievers, antihistamines, and bandages.

- Consider consulting a travel clinic for any recommended vaccinations and medications, such as antimalarials.

5. **Sun Protection**:

- Bora Bora enjoys plenty of sunshine, so packing sun protection items is crucial:

- **Sunscreen**: Bring a high SPF sunscreen to protect your skin from the strong tropical sun.

- **Sunglasses**: Polarized sunglasses will shield your eyes from the intense glare of the water.

- **Wide-Brimmed Hat**: A wide-brimmed hat will provide extra shade and protect your face and neck.

6. **Swimwear and Snorkeling Gear**:

- Bora Bora's clear waters are perfect for swimming and snorkeling. Be sure to pack swimwear, snorkeling masks, and fins. If you have your own snorkeling gear, consider bringing it for a more comfortable experience.

7. **Insect Repellent**:

- While Bora Bora doesn't have a severe mosquito problem, it's still a good idea to bring insect repellent for evenings or outdoor activities.

8. **Light Clothing**:

- The tropical climate of Bora Bora means that light, breathable clothing is ideal. Pack comfortable clothing like shorts, T-shirts, and sundresses.

- Don't forget a light jacket for cooler evenings.

9. **Waterproof Bag and Dry Bags**:

- Protect your valuables, like your smartphone, wallet, and camera, with a waterproof bag or a dry bag. These will be handy for water-based activities and excursions.

10. **Footwear**:

- In addition to comfortable walking shoes or sandals for exploring the island, consider water shoes or reef shoes.

11. **Camera and Underwater Camera**:

- Bora Bora's picturesque landscapes and vibrant marine life make it a photographer's paradise. Bring a camera or a waterproof action camera to capture your memories.

12. **Travel Locks and Security**:

- Use travel locks to secure your luggage, and consider a portable safe for valuable items in your accommodations.

By packing these travel essentials, you'll be well-prepared to make the most of your Bora Bora experience.

Things to know before you travel to Bora Bora

Here are some essential things you should know to make your trip enjoyable and hassle-free:

1. **Climate and Weather**:

- Bora Bora has a tropical climate with warm temperatures year-round. Be prepared for occasional rain showers, especially during the wet season from November to April. Don't forget to pack sunscreen and insect repellent.

2. **Language**:

- The official languages in French Polynesia are French and Tahitian. English is also widely spoken, particularly in the tourism industry. Learning a few basic French or Tahitian phrases can be helpful and appreciated.

3. **Local Time**:

- Bora Bora operates on Tahiti Time, which is 10 hours behind Coordinated Universal Time (UTC-10:00).

4. **Dress Code**:

- Bora Bora has a relaxed dress code, but when visiting non-beach areas or dining in upscale restaurants, it's respectful to wear modest clothing. Pack swimwear, casual clothing, and a light jacket for cooler evenings.

5. **Environmental Conservation**:

- Bora Bora is known for its pristine natural beauty. Respect the environment, follow local conservation efforts, and do not disturb marine life.

6. **Local Customs**:

- Respect local customs and traditions, such as covering up when visiting non-beach areas and showing respect in sacred or religious sites.

7. **Island Time**:

- Bora Bora operates on a relaxed and unhurried schedule known as "island time." Embrace the laid-back attitude and go with the flow during your stay.

8. **Respect for the Locals**:

- Be polite and respectful to the local people. Learn about their culture and engage in a friendly manner with residents.

By keeping these tips in mind, you can ensure a smooth and unforgettable journey to Bora Bora, one of the world's most sought-after travel destinations.

Chapter 4

Additional tips

Local customs and etiquette of Bora Bora

Here are some key customs and etiquette tips for Bora Bora:

1. **Greetings and Politeness**:

- Politeness and respect are highly valued in Bora Bora. Always greet locals with a friendly "Ia ora na" (pronounced 'yo-rah-nah'), which means "hello" or "good health" in Tahitian. Using basic Tahitian phrases like "mauruuru" (thank you) is appreciated.

2. **Modest Dress**:

- While Bora Bora has a relaxed dress code, it's respectful to cover up when visiting non-beach areas, including restaurants and local communities. Keep swimwear for the beach and pool areas.

3. **Respect Religious Sites**:

- French Polynesia, including Bora Bora, has a strong Christian influence. When visiting churches or religious sites, dress modestly and act respectfully.

Always ask for permission before taking photos inside religious buildings.

4. **Tipping**:

- Tipping is not a common practice in French Polynesia, but it is appreciated. If you receive exceptional service, consider leaving a small tip. However, it's not obligatory.

5. **Gift Giving**:

- If you are invited to a local's home, it's polite to bring a small gift, such as a local souvenir or fruits.

6. **No Public Nudity**:

- Public nudity, including topless sunbathing, is not acceptable in Bora Bora. Always wear appropriate swimwear on public beaches.

7. **Gifting Flowers**:

- Gifting flowers, especially tiare or gardenia blossoms, is a common and appreciated gesture in Tahitian culture. Flowers are often worn behind the ear as a sign of welcome.

8. **Shoes in Homes**:

- When visiting someone's home, it is customary to remove your shoes before entering. This practice is common in many Polynesian cultures.

9. **Cultural Sensitivity**:

- Bora Bora's cultural heritage is rich and diverse. Show respect for local customs and traditions, and ask for guidance when engaging in cultural activities or ceremonies.

10. **Conservation Efforts**:

- Bora Bora is actively involved in conservation and environmental protection. Support these efforts by participating in eco-friendly activities and reducing your environmental impact.

11. **Learn about the Culture**:

- Take the opportunity to learn about the local culture, traditions, and history. Engage with local residents, visit cultural centers, and attend traditional performances to gain a deeper understanding of the island's heritage.

By following these customs and etiquette tips, you can show respect for the local culture and contribute to a positive and culturally sensitive experience in Bora Bora.

Safety and emergency information

Bora Bora is generally a safe destination, like any other place, it's important to be aware of safety guidelines and have a plan in case of unexpected situations. Here is some safety and emergency information for your trip to Bora Bora:

1. **Health and Medical Services**:

- Bora Bora has a small hospital, the Centre Hospitalier de Bora Bora, which can handle minor medical issues. For more serious medical conditions, patients may be transferred to Tahiti.

- It's advisable to have travel insurance that covers medical emergencies, including evacuation to Tahiti if needed.

2. **Emergency Services**:

- The emergency phone number in Bora Bora is 15 for medical assistance and 17 for police. Keep these numbers handy.

- In case of a medical emergency, you may need to arrange transportation to the local hospital or, if necessary, a transfer to Tahiti for advanced medical care.

3. **Crime and Safety**:

- Bora Bora is generally a safe destination with a low crime rate. However, petty theft and burglaries can occur, so take precautions to secure your belongings, especially in crowded areas.

- Use hotel room safes to store valuable items and documents.

4. **Natural Disasters**:

- French Polynesia, including Bora Bora, is prone to natural disasters such as cyclones (tropical storms or hurricanes) and tropical depressions. The cyclone season typically runs from November to April. If you plan to visit during this period, stay informed about weather conditions and follow local advisories.

5. **Emergency Evacuation Plan**:

- Be aware of your accommodation's emergency evacuation plan. Familiarize yourself with escape routes and emergency contact information.

Chapter 5

Accommodation options

Bora Bora offers a range of accommodation options that cater to various budgets and preferences. Here are some accommodation options to consider:

1. **Overwater Bungalows**:

- Overwater bungalows are the iconic accommodation choice in Bora Bora. These luxurious, private villas are built directly over the lagoon, offering direct access to the crystal-clear waters.

2. **Beachfront Resorts**:

- Beachfront resorts in Bora Bora provide direct access to the island's beautiful beaches and stunning views of the lagoon.

3. **Luxury Hotels and Villas**:

- Apart from overwater bungalows, you can find luxurious suites and villas on the island. These accommodations often come with private pools, beautiful gardens, and top-notch amenities.

4. **Boutique Hotels and Guesthouses**:

- Bora Bora also has boutique hotels and guesthouses that offer a more intimate and authentic experience. These options are often more affordable.

5. **Vacation Rentals and Villas**:

- If you prefer self-catering or traveling with a group, vacation rentals and villas are available for rent. You can find them on various booking platforms.

6. **Budget Accommodations**:

- While Bora Bora is known for luxury, budget travelers can find affordable options. These may include smaller hotels or guesthouses.

7. **Camping**:

- Camping is not a common form of accommodation in Bora Bora due to its remote location and luxury-focused tourism. However, some campgrounds may be available on neighboring islands if you're open to exploring beyond Bora Bora.

When choosing accommodation in Bora Bora, consider your budget, travel style, and desired amenities. Keep in mind that Bora Bora is a popular destination, and it's advisable to book accommodations well in advance, especially during the high season (June to August and December to March).

Overwater Bungalows

1. **Four Seasons Resort Bora Bora**

- **Address**: Motu Tehotu, Bora Bora, French Polynesia

- **Offerings**: Overwater bungalows with stunning lagoon views, private plunge pools, and direct water access. World-class dining, spa, and water activities.

- **Price Range**: Overwater bungalows typically range from $1,000 to $2,500 per night.

2. **St. Regis Bora Bora Resort**

- **Address**: Motu Ome'e BP 506, Bora Bora, French Polynesia

- **Offerings**: Luxurious overwater villas with butler service, private terraces, and glass floors to observe marine life below. Gourmet dining and a serene spa.

- **Price Range**: Overwater villas typically range from $1,200 to $2,500 per night.

3. **Conrad Bora Bora Nui**

- **Address**: BP 502, Vaitape, Bora Bora, French Polynesia

- **Offerings**: Overwater bungalows and villas with private decks, infinity pools, and panoramic ocean views. Multiple dining options and a full-service spa.

- **Price Range**: Overwater accommodations typically range from $900 to $2,000 per night.

4. **InterContinental Bora Bora Resort & Thalasso Spa**

- **Address**: Motu Piti Aau, Bora Bora, French Polynesia

- **Offerings**: Overwater suites with glass-bottom coffee tables, private sundecks, and direct lagoon access. Exceptional spa and fine dining.

- **Price Range**: Overwater suites typically range from $800 to $1,800 per night.

5. **Le Meridien Bora Bora**

- **Address**: Motu Tape, BP 190, Bora Bora, French Polynesia

- **Offerings**: Overwater bungalows with glass floors, private lagoon access, and magnificent views. An in-house turtle sanctuary and water sports.

- **Price Range**: Overwater bungalows typically range from $700 to $1,500 per night.

6. **The Brando**

- **Address**: Tetiaroa, Arue, French Polynesia

- **Offerings**: Luxury villas on a private island, all-inclusive packages, fine dining, spa, and eco-friendly activities.

- **Price Range**: Luxury accommodations typically range from $2,500 to $10,000+ per night.

Boutique Hotels and Guesthouses

1. **Oa Oa Lodge**

- **Address**: Matira Point, Bora Bora, French Polynesia

- **Offerings**: Charming bungalows, garden setting, and a relaxed atmosphere. Close to Matira Beach.

- **Price Range**: Boutique bungalows typically range from $200 to $400 per night.

2. **Fare Pea Iti**

- **Address**: Vaitape, Bora Bora, French Polynesia

- **Offerings**: Cozy guesthouse, Polynesian-style rooms, and a friendly ambiance. Near the main village.

- **Price Range**: Guesthouse rooms typically range from $150 to $350 per night.

3. **Sunset Hill Lodge**

- **Address**: Bora Bora, French Polynesia

- **Offerings**: Intimate lodge, panoramic views, and a tranquil location. Ideal for couples seeking a quiet retreat.

- **Price Range**: Lodge rooms typically range from $250 to $450 per night.

4. **Villa Rea Hanaa**

- **Address**: Vaitape, Bora Bora, French Polynesia

- **Offerings**: Polynesian guesthouse, traditional bungalows, and a warm welcome. Close to amenities and attractions.

- **Price Range**: Guesthouse rooms typically range from $200 to $400 per night.

5. **Vaitape Guest House**

- **Address**: Vaitape, Bora Bora, French Polynesia

- **Offerings**: Cozy guesthouse, friendly hosts, and proximity to the village and waterfront.

- **Price Range**: Guesthouse rooms typically range from $150 to $300 per night.

Vacation Rentals and Villas

1. **Bora Bora Beach House**

- **Address**: Bora Bora, French Polynesia

- **Offerings**: Private beachfront villa with multiple bedrooms, fully equipped kitchen, and outdoor spaces. Ideal for families or groups.

- **Price Range**: Rental rates typically range from $600 to $1,200+ per night.

2. **Villa Bora Bora**

- **Address**: Matira Point, Bora Bora, French Polynesia

- **Offerings**: Luxurious beachfront villa, infinity pool, and modern amenities. Great for a private getaway.

- **Price Range**: Rental rates typically range from $800 to $1,500+ per night.

3. **Blue Heaven Island**

- **Address**: Bora Bora, French Polynesia

- **Offerings**: Private island rental with comfortable accommodations, water access, and tranquility. Perfect for a secluded escape.

- **Price Range**: Rental rates typically range from $500 to $1,000+ per night.

4. **Villa Faaopore**

- **Address**: Matira Point, Bora Bora, French Polynesia
- **Offerings**: Stylish villa with ocean views, well-equipped kitchen, and spacious living areas. Great for a family vacation.
- **Price Range**: Rental rates typically range from $500 to $1,200+ per night.

5. **Villa Moana**

- **Address**: Bora Bora, French Polynesia
- **Offerings**: Private beachfront villa with tropical gardens, outdoor dining, and direct lagoon access. Ideal for a romantic getaway.
- **Price Range**: Rental rates typically range from $600 to $1,200+ per night.

Please note that the price ranges provided are approximate and can vary based on factors such as the size of the accommodation, the time of year, and any additional services or amenities included in the rental. It's advisable to contact the property directly for the most up-to-date rates and availability. Enjoy your stay in Bora Bora!

Things to consider when deciding where to stay in Bora Bora

Choosing the right place to stay in Bora Bora is a crucial decision to make your trip memorable and enjoyable. The island offers a variety of accommodations, from luxurious overwater bungalows to budget-friendly options. Here are some key factors to consider when deciding where to stay in Bora Bora:

1. **Budget**:

- Determine your budget for accommodations. Bora Bora offers a wide range of options, so knowing your budget will help narrow down your choices.

2. **Accommodation Type**:

- Decide on the type of accommodation that suits your preferences. Choices include overwater bungalows, beachfront resorts, boutique hotels, vacation rentals, and more.

3. **Location**:

- Bora Bora is a relatively small island, but its accommodations are spread out. Consider whether you want to stay near the main village of Vaitape, on the main island (Motu Mute), or on a private motu (islet). Each location offers a different experience.

4. **Activities and Amenities**:

- Consider the activities and amenities offered by the accommodation. Some resorts include water sports, spa services, restaurants, and cultural experiences. Choose an option that aligns with your interests.

5. **Romance vs. Family-Friendly**:

- Bora Bora is a popular honeymoon destination, but it's also suitable for families. Some accommodations are more romantic and cater to couples, while others offer family-friendly activities and facilities.

6. **Privacy**:

- Determine how much privacy you want. Overwater bungalows are more private, but beachfront properties may have more public spaces and activities.

7. **Dining Options**:

- Check the dining options available at the accommodation. Some resorts have multiple restaurants and bars, while smaller properties may offer limited dining choices.

8. **All-Inclusive vs. À La Carte**:

- Decide whether you prefer an all-inclusive package or à la carte pricing. All-inclusive packages can simplify your budgeting, but they may be more expensive.

9. **Special Occasions**:

- If you're celebrating a special occasion, inform the accommodation in advance. Many resorts offer special packages for honeymooners or anniversaries.

10. **Reviews and Recommendations**:

- Read online reviews and seek recommendations from fellow travelers. These can provide valuable insights into the quality of accommodations.

11. **Accessibility**:

- If you have mobility concerns, consider accommodations with facilities and services that cater to your needs.

12. **Length of Stay**:

- Your length of stay in Bora Bora may influence your choice of accommodation. Longer stays might warrant a more diverse range of amenities and activities.

13. **Local Experiences**:

- Research accommodations that offer unique local experiences, such as cultural activities, traditional Polynesian dinners, or guided excursions.

Bora Bora offers a diverse array of accommodations to suit various tastes and preferences. Take your time to research and choose the one that aligns with your travel goals, whether it's a romantic getaway, a family vacation, or a solo adventure.

Chapter 6

Food and dining

Top Restaurants

Bora Bora, a jewel of the South Pacific, is renowned for its stunning landscapes, crystal-clear waters, and overwater bungalows. It's a destination where visitors can experience not only natural beauty but also exceptional cuisine. The island offers a range of dining options, from traditional Polynesian fare to gourmet international dishes. In this guide, we'll explore the top 10 best restaurants in Bora Bora, each with its unique offerings and approximate price range.

1. **Lagoon by Jean-Georges**

- **Address**: St. Regis Bora Bora Resort, Motu Ome'e BP 506, Bora Bora, French Polynesia

- **Description**: Lagoon by Jean-Georges is the epitome of luxury dining in Bora Bora. Located at the St. Regis Resort, the restaurant offers a fine dining experience with a menu curated by the renowned chef Jean-Georges Vongerichten. The dishes are a fusion of French and Asian flavors, with an emphasis on fresh, local ingredients. Guests can savor the exquisite cuisine while enjoying the breathtaking views of Mount Otemanu and the lagoon.

- **Price Range**: Approximately $200 to $400 per person for a three-course meal.

2. **Bloody Mary's**

- **Address**: Bora Bora, French Polynesia

- **Description**: Bloody Mary's is an iconic and laid-back restaurant in Bora Bora. Known for its rustic charm and relaxed atmosphere, it has been a favorite among locals and tourists for years. The menu primarily features fresh seafood, including fish, lobster, and clams, which guests can select from a display and have prepared to their liking. The open-air restaurant also offers a variety of tropical cocktails and a fun, sandy floor.

- **Price Range**: Approximately $60 to $100 per person for a seafood dinner.

3. **La Villa Mahana**

- **Address**: Fare Piti U'uta, Bora Bora, French Polynesia

- **Description**: La Villa Mahana is a romantic and intimate dining experience in Bora Bora. With only a few tables, the restaurant provides personalized service and a fine French cuisine-inspired menu.

Guests can enjoy creative dishes prepared by the chef using the freshest local ingredients.

- **Price Range**: Approximately $150 to $300 per person for a multi-course tasting menu.

4. **St. James Restaurant**

- **Address**: Le Meridien Bora Bora, Motu Tape, BP 190, Bora Bora, French Polynesia

- **Description**: St. James Restaurant is located at Le Meridien Resort and offers a blend of international and Polynesian cuisine. The restaurant provides a stunning setting overlooking the lagoon and Mount Otemanu. The menu includes a range of fresh seafood, local specialties, and international dishes. The restaurant also hosts theme nights featuring Polynesian dance performances.

- **Price Range**: Approximately $80 to $150 per person for a multi-course dinner.

5. **La Matira Beach Restaurant**

- **Address**: Matira Beach, Bora Bora, French Polynesia

- **Description**: La Matira Beach Restaurant is a charming and casual dining spot with an ideal location right on Matira Beach. Guests can enjoy their meals with their toes in the sand and panoramic views of the lagoon. The menu features a mix of French and Polynesian cuisine, including fresh seafood, tropical fruits, and local flavors.

- **Price Range**: Approximately $50 to $100 per person for a meal with a view.

6. **Kaina Hut**

- **Address**: Bora Bora, French Polynesia

- **Description**: Kaina Hut is a delightful beachfront restaurant that offers a diverse menu of local dishes, French cuisine, and international favorites. With its relaxed and friendly atmosphere, it's a popular choice among visitors looking for a casual dining experience. In addition to its food, Kaina Hut is known for its creative cocktails and fresh fruit juices.

- **Price Range**: Approximately $40 to $80 per person for a diverse menu.

7. **Matira Point Restaurant**

- **Address**: Matira Point, Bora Bora, French Polynesia

- **Description**: Matira Point Restaurant is a hidden gem in Bora Bora, offering a relaxed and scenic dining experience. Situated at the southern tip of the island, the restaurant provides picturesque views of the lagoon and is a great spot to watch the sunset. The menu includes a variety of seafood, meat, and vegetarian options, as well as an extensive wine list.

- **Price Range**: Approximately $60 to $120 per person for a memorable meal.

8. **Restaurant MaiKai Bora Bora**

- **Address**: Vaitape, Bora Bora, French Polynesia

- **Description**: Restaurant MaiKai is a local favorite that serves a mix of traditional Polynesian dishes and international cuisine. The open-air setting offers a pleasant and relaxed ambiance. The restaurant is known for its live music and dance performances that provide guests with a taste of Polynesian culture.

- **Price Range**: Approximately $40 to $80 per person for a diverse menu.

9. **Sushi Take**

- **Address**: Vaitape, Bora Bora, French Polynesia

- **Description**: Sushi Take is the go-to place for sushi lovers in Bora Bora. The restaurant offers a range of sushi and sashimi options, as well as other Japanese dishes. The sushi is prepared with fresh seafood, including local catches. It's a great choice for a lighter meal or a change of pace from traditional Polynesian fare.

- **Price Range**: Approximately $40 to $80 per person for a sushi dinner.

10. **MaiKai Bora Bora Beach Restaurant**

- **Address**: Plage Matira, Bora Bora, French Polynesia

- **Description**: MaiKai Beach Restaurant is another beachfront dining option with a focus on fresh seafood and Polynesian cuisine. Guests can enjoy their meals on the beach with their feet in the sand. The restaurant is known for its tropical cocktails and picturesque location.

- **Price Range**: Approximately $50 to $100 per person for a beachfront meal.

Please note that the price ranges provided are approximate and can vary based on factors such as the choice of dishes, drinks, and the specific restaurant's location. Additionally, some of the restaurants may offer fixed-price menus, theme nights, or special packages that can influence the overall cost of your dining experience. It's advisable to check with the restaurants for the most up-to-date menus and prices before planning your visit to Bora Bora. Enjoy your culinary journey on this beautiful island!

Best traditional foods to try in Bora bora

Bora Bora offers a delightful range of traditional Polynesian foods that showcase the flavors and culinary heritage of the islands. When visiting this tropical paradise, be sure to try these delicious traditional dishes:

1. **Poisson Cru**:

- Poisson cru is a Tahitian specialty and a must-try in Bora Bora. It's similar to ceviche, featuring fresh, raw fish (often tuna or mahi-mahi) marinated in coconut milk, lime juice, and vegetables. The combination of flavors is refreshing and delightful.

2. **I'a Ota**:

- I'a ota is another popular seafood dish. It consists of freshly caught fish, typically served with lime, coconut milk, vegetables, and spices. The fish is often marinated in the local hot sauce known as "mitihue."

3. **Firi Firi**:

- Firi firi is a popular Polynesian snack. These small, deep-fried doughnuts are sweet and doughy, often dusted with powdered sugar. They make for a tasty treat or dessert.

4. **Poisson Cru au Lait de Coco**:

- Similar to poisson cru, this variation includes coconut milk, giving it a creamier texture and richer flavor. The addition of coconut milk complements the lime juice and fresh fish perfectly.

5. **Ecrevisses a la vanille**:

- Ecrevisses, or freshwater crayfish, are commonly cooked with vanilla in Bora Bora. The vanilla imparts a sweet and aromatic flavor to the dish, which is often served with vegetables and rice.

6. **Fafa**:

- Fafa is a traditional Tahitian dish made from taro leaves and coconut milk. The leaves are cooked until tender and served as a side dish or main course, often accompanied by breadfruit.

7. **Fe'i**:

- Fe'i is a type of banana grown in Bora Bora and other Polynesian islands. It can be prepared in various ways, including roasting, boiling, or steaming, and is often served with local dishes.

8. **Poi**:

- Poi is a traditional Polynesian staple made from fermented taro root. It has a unique, tangy flavor and can be eaten as a side dish or dessert.

9. **Tamure**:

- Tamure is a traditional Tahitian dessert made from sweet potatoes and coconut cream. The sweet potatoes are mashed and blended with coconut cream, sugar, and vanilla for a delicious and satisfying treat.

When dining in Bora Bora, be sure to explore local eateries.

Budget Eateries in bora bora

Bora Bora is often associated with luxury and upscale dining, but there are budget-friendly dining options available on the island if you know where to look. Here are some budget eateries in Bora Bora:

1. **Food Trucks (Roulettes)**:

- The food trucks in Bora Bora, known as "roulettes," are an excellent choice for affordable and delicious meals. These mobile eateries offer a variety of dishes, including poisson cru, grilled fish, chicken, burgers, and more. You can find them in Vaitape, the main town, and around the island.

2. **Yummy Snack**:

- Yummy Snack is a popular food truck offering a range of affordable dishes, including Chinese and local Polynesian cuisine. Try their mahi-mahi with vanilla sauce, a local favorite.

3. **Matira Beach Snack**:

- Located near Matira Beach, this snack bar serves reasonably priced sandwiches, hamburgers, and crepes. It's a convenient spot to grab a quick meal during your beach day.

4. **Super U**:

- Super U is a supermarket in Vaitape where you can purchase groceries and snacks. You can pick up fresh fruits, sandwiches, and other budget-friendly items to enjoy during your stay.

5. **Kaina Hut**:

- Kaina Hut offers affordable takeaway and quick-service options, including poisson cru and grilled fish. It's a favorite spot for tourists looking for a taste of local cuisine.

6. **Bloody Mary's Bar & Grill**:

- While Bloody Mary's is known for its seafood and exotic cocktails, it also offers a more budget-friendly option. Try their "Burger Mary" for a more affordable dining experience.

7. **St. James Restaurant**:

- St. James Restaurant offers a mix of Polynesian and French cuisine. While it's not the cheapest option, it provides good value for the quality of food and service.

8. **Aloha Snackbar**:

- Located near Matira Beach, Aloha Snackbar offers casual and reasonably priced meals. Enjoy a pizza, crepe, or sandwich while taking in the beautiful beach views.

9. **Les Roulottes de Bora Bora**:

- Another set of food trucks located in Vaitape, Les Roulottes de Bora Bora, offers a variety of dishes, from grilled meats to pizza. You can find affordable options for dinner here.

10. **Vaitape Local Restaurants**:

- In Vaitape, the main town, there are several small local restaurants that serve Polynesian dishes. These establishments may offer more budget-friendly meals compared to those at upscale resorts.

When dining on a budget in Bora Bora, consider exploring local eateries and food trucks. While the island is known for luxury, these affordable options allow you to enjoy the flavors of French Polynesia without overspending.

Dietary Restrictions

Traveling to a destination like Bora Bora with dietary restrictions can be a concern, but with some preparation and communication, you can still enjoy your trip and savor local flavors. Here are some tips for travelers with dietary restrictions in Bora Bora:

1. **Communicate in Advance**:

- If you have dietary restrictions, it's essential to communicate them clearly to your accommodation and any dining establishments you plan to visit. Many resorts and restaurants are accommodating and can prepare meals to meet your needs.

2. **Learn Local Ingredients**:

- Familiarize yourself with local ingredients and dishes that are safe for your dietary restrictions. In Bora Bora, many dishes include fresh seafood, tropical fruits, and vegetables, making it possible to find suitable options.

3. **Pack Snacks**:

- If you have severe dietary restrictions or allergies, consider bringing some of your own snacks or pre-packaged meals to ensure you have options that meet your needs.

4. **Allergen Cards**:

- If you have food allergies, consider using allergen cards that clearly list the specific allergens you need to avoid in both English and the local language. This can help ensure that your dietary restrictions are understood.

5. **Resort Dining**:

- If you're staying at a resort, inform them in advance about your dietary restrictions. Most upscale resorts have experienced chefs who can create custom dishes for guests with specific needs.

6. **Fresh Fruits and Vegetables**:

- Bora Bora is known for its abundance of fresh fruits and vegetables. Take advantage of the local produce to create your own meals or request dishes made with fresh ingredients at local restaurants.

7. **Grilled Seafood**:

- For those with dietary restrictions like gluten intolerance, grilled seafood can be a safe and delicious option in Bora Bora. Many restaurants offer fresh catches of the day.

8. **Tropical Fruits**:

- Enjoy the tropical fruits of Bora Bora. These are widely available and can make for a delightful and safe snack or dessert option.

9. **Vegan and Vegetarian Options**:

- While vegan and vegetarian options may be limited in traditional Polynesian cuisine, you can often find plant-based dishes like salads, vegetable stir-fries, and fruit platters.

10. **Be Cautious with Sauces and Condiments**:

- Be aware that some local sauces and condiments may contain ingredients that don't meet your dietary restrictions. It's a good idea to inquire about ingredients when dining out.

By taking these precautions and being proactive in communicating your dietary restrictions, you can still enjoy your trip to Bora Bora while adhering to your specific dietary needs.

Chapter 7

family activities

Couples in Bora Bora

Bora Bora is renowned for its romantic atmosphere and stunning natural beauty, making it an ideal destination for couples. While there are plenty of traditional romantic activities to enjoy, such as sunset dinners and strolls along the pristine beaches, there are also some unusual and unique experiences that can make your trip even more memorable. Here are some fun and romantic things for couples to do in Bora Bora:

1. **Shark and Ray Feeding Excursion**:

- Join a guided excursion to feed and swim with black-tip reef sharks and stingrays in their natural habitat. It's a thrilling and unique adventure that allows you to get up close with these incredible marine creatures.

2. **Private Lagoon Picnic**:

- Arrange for a private picnic on a secluded motu (islet) in the lagoon. Enjoy a romantic meal surrounded by the beauty of Bora Bora, complete with a picnic basket and a breathtaking view.

3. **Stargazing from an Overwater Bungalow**:

- Bora Bora's remote location and minimal light pollution make it an excellent place for stargazing. Enjoy a quiet evening on your overwater bungalow deck, gazing at the clear night sky with your loved one.

4. **Sunset Sail**:

- While a sunset cruise is a classic romantic activity, consider booking a private sunset sail for a more intimate experience. Enjoy the changing colors of the sky as you relax on the deck of a sailing boat.

5. **Underwater Helmet Walk**:

- Experience a unique underwater adventure by taking an underwater helmet walk. Walk hand in hand on the ocean floor and discover the vibrant marine life while staying dry in a helmet with a clear visor.

6. **Couple's Spa Treatment**:

- Many resorts offer unique couple's spa treatments. Enjoy a side-by-side massage or a spa ritual in an overwater bungalow, complete with tranquil lagoon views.

7. **Polynesian Dance Class**:

- Join a Polynesian dance class together to learn the traditional dance moves and rhythms. It's a fun and cultural experience that can add a unique element to your trip.

8. **Romantic Canoe Breakfast**:

- Some resorts offer a romantic breakfast delivered to your overwater bungalow via outrigger canoe. Enjoy a delicious meal as you float on the crystal-clear waters of the lagoon.

9. **Private Helicopter Tour**:

- Get a bird's-eye view of the stunning landscapes of Bora Bora with a private helicopter tour. The unique perspective will provide you with a deeper appreciation of the island's beauty.

10. **Vanilla Farm Tour**:

- Explore a vanilla plantation on the island and learn about the cultivation and processing of vanilla beans. Discover the rich aroma and flavors of Tahitian vanilla as a couple.

11. **Tahitian Marriage Blessing**:

- Experience a traditional Tahitian wedding blessing ceremony, complete with Polynesian customs, flower crowns, and an authentic celebration of love and commitment.

These unique and romantic experiences in Bora Bora will create lasting memories and enhance your connection as a couple.

Bora Bora with kids

Bora Bora is also a fantastic destination for families with children. Here are some of the best fun activities for kids to do in Bora Bora:

Glass-Bottom Boat Tours:

- Take a glass-bottom boat tour to explore the vibrant underwater world of Bora Bora without getting wet. Kids will be thrilled to see colorful coral reefs, tropical fish, and other marine life through the glass floor of the boat. It's a safe and exciting adventure for children of all ages.

Turtle Sanctuary Visit:

- Visit the Bora Bora Turtle Center, where kids can learn about marine conservation efforts and interact with rescued sea turtles. It's both educational and heartwarming for children to see these majestic creatures up close.

Shark and Ray Feeding Tours:

- Join a guided excursion to feed black-tip reef sharks and stingrays. Kids can participate in the feeding and watch the graceful movements of these fascinating creatures.

Dolphin Watching Tours:

- Take a family boat tour to spot dolphins playing in the lagoon. These intelligent and friendly animals often swim alongside the boats, providing a thrilling experience for children.

Family Photography Session: Capture your family's memories with a professional photography session against the backdrop of Bora Bora's stunning landscapes. It's a great way to create lasting mementos of your trip.

Mini Golf: - Some resorts on the island offer mini golf, which can be a fun and lighthearted activity for kids and families to enjoy together.

Boat Rides and Island Hopping: - Consider taking boat rides to explore nearby islands and motus. Each island has its own unique charm, and kids will enjoy the excitement of island hopping and discovering new places.

Chapter 8

Best beaches in Bora Bora

Bora Bora is renowned for its stunning beaches, each with its own unique charm and beauty. Here are some of the best beaches in Bora Bora:

1. Matira Beach:

- Matira Beach is arguably the most famous and one of the best beaches in Bora Bora. It features soft, powdery white sand and clear, shallow waters. The beach is an excellent place for swimming, sunbathing, and watching the sunset. It's also home to some beachfront restaurants and resorts.

2. Matira Point:

- Located near Matira Beach, Matira Point offers stunning views of the surrounding lagoon and ocean. The point is a popular spot for watching the sunset, and its rocky shoreline provides an excellent backdrop for photos.

3. Coral Gardens:

- While not a traditional beach, Coral Gardens is a fantastic snorkeling spot where you can swim among colorful coral formations and a diverse array of marine life. It's an underwater paradise accessible by boat.

4. Sofitel Private Beach:

- The Sofitel Private Beach is exclusive to guests of the Sofitel Bora Bora Private Island Resort. This small, pristine beach is perfect for those seeking solitude and tranquility.

5. Matira Bay:

- Matira Bay is another beautiful stretch of beach near Matira Beach. It's an excellent place for swimming and enjoying the lagoon's warm waters. The shallow depth of the bay makes it family-friendly.

6. Pofai Bay Beach:

- Located in Vaitape, Pofai Bay Beach is a convenient option for those staying in the main town. It provides a place to relax by the water, swim, and enjoy views of the lagoon.

7. Faanui Bay Beach:

- Faanui Bay Beach offers a more secluded and peaceful atmosphere. This beach is perfect for a quiet getaway, picnics, and exploring the natural surroundings.

8. Anau Beach:

- Anau Beach is known for its lush vegetation and proximity to Matira Beach. It offers an alternative spot to enjoy the breathtaking Bora Bora scenery.

9. Viatape Beach:

- Viatape Beach is close to the main village of Vaitape. While it may not be the most pristine beach, it's conveniently located and offers glimpses of local life and culture.

Top shopping areas in Bora Bora

Here are the top shopping areas in Bora Bora:

1. **Vaitape**:

- Vaitape is the main town on the island and serves as the primary commercial hub. Here, you'll find a variety of shops, boutiques, and markets where you can purchase souvenirs, clothing, jewelry, and local crafts. Look for Tahitian black pearls, local artwork, and colorful pareos (sarongs).

2. **Matira Point**:

- Matira Point has a small shopping area with boutiques and shops offering local handicrafts, black pearls, and clothing.

3. **Hotels and Resorts**:

- Many of the upscale hotels and resorts in Bora Bora have their own boutiques and shops. These on-site shops offer a selection of high-quality items, including jewelry, clothing, and beachwear. While prices can be higher, the convenience is unmatched.

4. **Black Pearl Shops**:

- Bora Bora is famous for its Tahitian black pearls, and there are numerous shops dedicated to these lustrous gems. Look for reputable black pearl shops where you can browse and purchase these precious gems, often set in jewelry.

5. **La Maison de la Vanille**:

- If you're a fan of vanilla, don't miss La Maison de la Vanille in Vaitape. Here, you can purchase a variety of vanilla products, from beans and extracts to cosmetics and fragrances.

Shopping in Bora Bora is more about finding unique, locally made products and souvenirs rather than luxury brands or extensive retail areas.

Chapter 9

Outdoor and nature experiences

Bora Bora offers a variety of outdoor activities for those who love to explore the island's natural beauty.

Hiking and Nature Trails:

1. **Mount Otemanu Hike**:

- The tallest peak on the island, Mount Otemanu, offers a challenging hike with breathtaking panoramic views. The journey is not for the faint-hearted, but the sense of accomplishment and the vistas from the top are well worth the effort.

2. **Mount Pahia Hike**:

- Slightly less demanding than Mount Otemanu, Mount Pahia provides a fantastic hiking opportunity. The trail takes you through lush vegetation and rewards you with spectacular views of the lagoon.

3. **Anau Hike**:

- The Anau area features several hiking trails that allow you to explore the island's interior. It's a great way to discover the local flora and fauna while immersing yourself in the island's natural beauty.

4. **Fa'anui Valley Hike**:

- The Fa'anui Valley hike is an enchanting experience, taking you through dense jungle and up to a viewpoint with stunning vistas of Bora Bora's lush landscape.

5. **Matira Point Trail**:

- This relatively easy trail offers stunning coastal views and opportunities for birdwatching. You can enjoy a leisurely walk while taking in the natural beauty of Matira Point.

6. **Bora Bora Lagoon Trail**:

- The Lagoon Trail is a gentle, scenic walk along the coastline, starting from Matira Beach and ending near Sofitel Private Island Resort. It's perfect for a relaxed hike with gorgeous lagoon views.

7. **Faanui Bay Lookout Trail**:

- Enjoy a pleasant hike to the Faanui Bay Lookout for incredible views of the bay, lush vegetation, and a sense of serenity away from the busier tourist areas.

Water Sports:

1. **Snorkeling**:

- Bora Bora's lagoon is teeming with marine life and coral reefs. Snorkeling is one of the most popular water activities, and you can rent equipment from various operators.

2. **Scuba Diving**:

- Explore the deeper waters of Bora Bora by going scuba diving. You'll have the chance to see colorful fish, rays, sharks, and even shipwrecks.

3. **Paddleboarding**:

- Stand-up paddleboarding is a fun and relatively easy water sport that allows you to explore the lagoon while standing on a board and using a paddle.

4. **Kiteboarding**:

- Bora Bora's steady trade winds make it an excellent destination for kiteboarding. You can take lessons or rent equipment to ride the waves and enjoy the thrill of this sport.

5. **Windsurfing**:

- The lagoon's gentle waves and consistent wind make it an ideal spot for windsurfing. Rentals and lessons are available for windsurfers of all levels.

6. **Jet Ski Tours**:

- Explore the lagoon on a guided jet ski tour. It's an exhilarating way to see the island's natural beauty from the water.

7. **Parasailing**:

- Get a bird's-eye view of Bora Bora by parasailing. You'll be harnessed to a parachute and lifted into the sky for a memorable experience.

Cycling and Biking:

1. **Cycling Around the Island**:

- Bora Bora has a scenic coastal road that's great for cycling. Rent a bicycle and enjoy a leisurely ride around the island, taking in the breathtaking views.

2. **Bike Tours**:

- Join a guided bike tour to explore the island's hidden gems and cultural sites. You'll have the opportunity to learn about Bora Bora's history and traditions while cycling.

3. **Mountain Biking**:

- For more adventurous cyclists, mountain biking is an option. You can explore the island's lush interior and hilly terrain on designated trails.

4. **Beach Cruisers**:

- Many resorts offer beach cruisers for guests to use. Take a relaxed ride along the coastal roads, stopping at beaches and viewpoints along the way.

5. **Eco-Friendly Electric Bikes**:

- Some bike rental shops offer eco-friendly electric bikes. These bikes can help you explore the island with less effort, making it suitable for all fitness levels.

6. **Motu Piti Aau Cycling**:

- Rent a bike and explore Motu Piti Aau, a small islet located near Bora Bora. You'll find a mix of beaches and beautiful natural scenery.

Bora Bora's diverse outdoor activities allow you to explore the island's lush landscapes, pristine waters, and tranquil settings.

Nightlife in Bora bora

Here's an overview of the nightlife in Bora Bora:

1. **Beachfront Dinners**:

- Dining by the beach is a popular and romantic evening activity in Bora Bora. Many restaurants, especially those located at resorts, offer beachfront dining with candlelit tables and the sound of lapping waves. It's a lovely way to enjoy a special dinner with your loved one.

2. **Tahitian Dance Shows**:

- While not traditional nightclubs, some dining establishments offer Tahitian dance shows during dinner service. These shows provide a cultural experience with vibrant music, dance, and storytelling.

3. **Stargazing**:

- Due to the island's remote location and minimal light pollution, Bora Bora is a fantastic place for stargazing. Some resorts offer stargazing experiences where you can marvel at the night sky and learn about the constellations.

4. **Private Dinner on the Beach**:

- Some resorts and tour operators offer the option to have a private dinner set up on the beach. This can be a wonderfully romantic experience, complete with a personal chef and server.

5. **Island Excursions**:

- Some evening excursions take you to explore the island's natural beauty at night. This can include sunset hikes, night snorkeling, or paddleboarding under the moonlight.

It's important to note that Bora Bora's nightlife is relatively quiet and subdued compared to larger cities and party destinations. The island's charm lies in its natural beauty and laid-back atmosphere. You are more likely to enjoy a leisurely and romantic evening rather than a vibrant and lively nightlife.

Conclusion and further resources for planning your trip to Bora bora

In conclusion, Bora Bora is a tropical paradise that offers a wide range of activities and experiences for travelers of all types. Whether you're seeking a romantic getaway, a family adventure, or a solo escape, this Polynesian island has something to offer. From its pristine beaches and clear lagoons to its lush hiking trails and thrilling water sports, Bora Bora provides a diverse and enchanting array of natural beauty and cultural experiences.

To ensure you have a memorable and well-planned trip to Bora Bora, it's essential to do thorough research and preparation. Here are some further resources and tips for planning your trip:

1. Official Tourism Websites:

- Visit the official tourism websites for Bora Bora and French Polynesia to access information on accommodations, activities, and travel guidelines.

2. Travel Forums and Communities:

- Join online travel forums and communities where you can ask questions, seek advice, and connect with fellow travelers who have visited Bora Bora. Websites like TripAdvisor and Lonely Planet's Thorn Tree Forum can be helpful.

3. Travel Agencies and Tour Operators:

- Consider working with travel agencies and tour operators that specialize in French Polynesia. They can help you plan and customize your trip, including accommodations, activities, and transportation.

4. Health and Safety:

- Check the latest health and safety guidelines, including vaccinations, travel insurance, and local regulations. The island is relatively safe, but it's wise to stay informed.

5. Timing and Seasons: - Consider the best time to visit Bora Bora based on your preferences. High season is from May to October, with dry weather and pleasant temperatures, while the wet season from November to April offers lower prices but the possibility of rain.

6. Reservations: - Make reservations for accommodations and activities well in advance, especially if you plan to visit during the high season. Popular overwater bungalows and tours tend to fill up quickly.

7. Local Customs and Etiquette: - Familiarize yourself with the local customs and etiquette of Bora Bora, including the respectful approach to the island's culture and environment.

8. Documentation: - Ensure you have all the necessary travel documentation, including a valid passport and any required visas. Double-check the entry requirements for French Polynesia.

9. Itinerary Planning: - Create a detailed itinerary to make the most of your time in Bora Bora. Balance your days with relaxation, adventure, and cultural experiences.

Bora Bora is a destination that lives up to its reputation as one of the world's most beautiful and idyllic places. With proper planning and preparation, you can make the most of your trip to this tropical paradise, creating memories that will last a lifetime.

Appendices

Glossary of Local Phrases

While the primary language spoken in Bora Bora is French, the local culture is also deeply influenced by the Tahitian language and customs. Here are some common local phrases and words you may encounter during your visit to Bora Bora:

1. **Ia Orana** - "Hello" or "Greetings" in Tahitian.

2. **Maeva** - "Welcome" in Tahitian.

3. **Nana** - "Goodbye" or "See you later" in Tahitian.

4. **Mauruuru** - "Thank you" in Tahitian.

5. **Aroha** - "Love" in Tahitian.

6. **Fare** - "House" or "Home" in Tahitian.

7. **Motu** - "Islet" or "Small Island" in Tahitian.

8. **Marae** - An ancient Polynesian temple or sacred site.

9. **Tere Fa'ati** - A traditional feast or meal in Tahitian culture.

10. **Havaiki** - A Tahitian concept of a paradise or a place of bliss.

11. **Fenua** - "Land" or "Country" in Tahitian.

12. **Mana** - A spiritual force or power often associated with nature.

13. **Vahine** - "Woman" in Tahitian.

14. **Tane** - "Man" in Tahitian.

15. **Fare Manihini** - A guesthouse or accommodations in Tahitian.

16. **I'oa** - A traditional name in Tahitian culture.

17. **Tere Vaa** - Outrigger canoeing, a popular activity in Bora Bora.

18. **Poe** - A traditional Tahitian dessert made from banana and taro.

19. **Tahua** - A Tahitian priest or spiritual leader.

20. **'Ava'e** - "Foot" in Tahitian.

21. **Fa'afaite** - "Adventure" in Tahitian.

22. **Moana** - "Ocean" in Tahitian.

23. **Pae pae** - "Lagoon" or "Reef" in Tahitian.

24. **Tupa'i** - "Island" or "Rock" in Tahitian.

25. **Reva** - "Dream" or "Vision" in Tahitian.

26. **Fenua'aihere** - "Wilderness" or "Unspoiled land" in Tahitian.

27. **'Ahi ma'a** - An underground oven used for traditional Tahitian cooking.

28. **Miti** - "Sea" or "Saltwater" in Tahitian.

Tahitian culture is deeply rooted in the daily life of Bora Bora, and understanding these phrases can help you connect with the local community and embrace the spirit of the island.

Useful Contacts

During your trip to Bora Bora, it's essential to have access to important contacts and resources to ensure a smooth and enjoyable experience. Here are some useful contacts you should keep on hand:

Emergency Contacts:

1. **Police**: In case of emergencies, including theft or safety concerns, dial the local police at 17.

2. **Fire Department**: For fire-related emergencies, contact the local fire department at 18.

3. **Medical Emergencies**: In the event of a medical emergency, you can reach the Bora Bora Hospital at +689 40 67 70 00. It's important to have travel insurance for healthcare coverage.

Transportation Services:

4. **Bora Bora Airport**: If you need assistance or information related to your flight, contact Bora Bora Airport at +689 40 67 70 14.

5. **Boat Transfers**: Many travelers use boat transfers to reach their accommodations. Keep the contact information for your boat transfer service or resort handy.

Accommodations:

6. **Your Accommodation**: Always have the contact information for your chosen accommodation, including the front desk or concierge, in case you need assistance during your stay.

Local Services:

7. **Bora Bora Tourism Information**: For information on local attractions, activities, and events, contact the Bora Bora Tourism Office at +689 40 67 70 84 or visit their website.

8. **Local Tour Operators**: If you've booked tours or activities, keep the contact information for the tour operators, including any pickup and drop-off details.

Embassy or Consulate:

9. **Your Country's Embassy or Consulate**: In case of emergencies, such as lost passports or legal issues, have the contact information for your country's embassy or consulate in French Polynesia.

Travel Insurance Provider:

10. **Travel Insurance Provider**: Keep the contact information for your travel insurance provider, including policy numbers, in case you need to make a claim or seek assistance during your trip.

Currency Exchange and Banking:

11. **Local Banks**: Know the operating hours and contact information for local banks or ATMs in case you need to access or exchange currency.

Local Contacts and Friends:

12. **Local Contacts**: If you have local friends or acquaintances in Bora Bora, ensure you have their contact information in case you need assistance or recommendations.

Language Assistance:

13. **Translation Services**: If you are not fluent in French or Tahitian, consider having a translation app or service on your phone for communication.

Tourist Helpline:

14. **Tourist Helpline**: Some destinations have dedicated tourist helplines, so check if Bora Bora has one, and keep the number for inquiries or assistance.

Before your trip, it's a good idea to make both physical and digital copies of important documents, such as your passport, travel insurance, and itinerary. Store these copies in a secure location separate from the originals and consider using a cloud-based storage solution for added security.

By having these useful contacts readily available, you can ensure a safer and more organized trip to Bora Bora, knowing that you have access to the resources you may need during your stay in this breathtaking paradise.

Sample Itineraries

Certainly! Here are three sample itineraries for various durations of stay in Bora Bora, each catering to different traveler preferences. Bora Bora offers a mix of adventure, relaxation, and romance, so you can tailor your itinerary to suit your interests.

Sample 3-Day Itinerary: Bora Bora Adventure Getaway

Day 1: Arrival and Water Adventures

- Morning: Arrive at Bora Bora Airport and transfer to your chosen accommodation.

- Afternoon: Start your adventure with a jet ski tour around the island. Explore the lagoon, visit the Coral Gardens, and spot marine life.

- Evening: Enjoy a beachfront dinner at your resort or at a local restaurant in Vaitape.

Day 2: Hiking and Cultural Experiences

- Morning: Hike Mount Pahia or Mount Otemanu for stunning panoramic views of Bora Bora.

- Afternoon: Visit a local marae (Tahitian temple) to learn about the island's history and culture.

- Evening: Attend a traditional Tahitian dance show and enjoy a Polynesian feast at your resort.

Day 3: Water Sports and Departure

- Morning: Try snorkeling in the vibrant coral gardens and swim with sharks and rays on a guided tour.

- Afternoon: Spend your afternoon paddleboarding or kayaking in the crystal-clear waters.

- Evening: Depart from Bora Bora, but not before capturing the last sunset over the lagoon.

Sample 5-Day Itinerary: Bora Bora Romantic Retreat

Day 1: Arrival and Relaxation

- Morning: Arrive at Bora Bora Airport and transfer to your overwater bungalow.

- Afternoon: Relax by the beach or your resort's pool and unwind from your journey.

- Evening: Enjoy a romantic dinner on your private deck, savoring the stunning sunset.

Day 2: Water Activities and Spa

- Morning: Begin your day with a leisurely snorkeling session around your bungalow, admiring the underwater world.

- Afternoon: Treat yourselves to a couple's massage or spa treatment at your resort.

- Evening: Savor a romantic dinner at one of the island's beachfront restaurants.

Day 3: Private Lagoon Tour

- Morning: Embark on a private lagoon tour by outrigger canoe or boat, exploring hidden coves and motus.

- Afternoon: Enjoy a picnic on a secluded beach and snorkel with colorful fish.

- Evening: Dine at your resort's overwater restaurant, with the ocean beneath you.

Day 4: Island Exploration and Sunset Cruise

- Morning: Rent a bicycle to explore the island's coastal roads and visit local villages.

- Afternoon: Join a sunset cruise for a romantic evening on the water.

- Evening: Relish a special sunset dinner on board or at a beachfront venue.

Day 5: Departure

- Morning: Enjoy a leisurely breakfast in your overwater bungalow.

- Afternoon: Spend your last few hours on the island relaxing on the beach or indulging in water activities.

- Evening: Depart from Bora Bora with beautiful memories of your romantic escape.

Sample 7-Day Itinerary: Bora Bora Family Adventure

Day 1: Arrival and Orientation

- Morning: Arrive at Bora Bora Airport and transfer to your family-friendly resort.

- Afternoon: Familiarize yourself with the resort's amenities, and let the kids play in the shallow lagoon.

- Evening: Have a relaxed family dinner at the resort's restaurant.

Day 2: Water Sports and Beach Time

- Morning: Start the day with snorkeling and water sports at the resort's beach.

- Afternoon: Enjoy a family beach picnic and build sandcastles.

- Evening: Participate in a cultural show and Polynesian buffet at your resort.

Day 3: Lagoon Exploration

- Morning: Go on a family-friendly lagoon tour, visiting Coral Gardens and swimming with sharks and rays.

- Afternoon: Take the kids on a glass-bottom boat tour to see the marine life.

- Evening: Dine at a casual local restaurant in Vaitape.

Day 4: Family Hike and Picnic

- Morning: Hike Matira Point with the family, enjoying scenic views.

- Afternoon: Have a picnic lunch at Matira Beach and let the kids play in the gentle waves.

- Evening: Order room service and relax in your bungalow.

*Day 5: Nature and Wildlife**

- Morning: Visit the Turtle Center to learn about sea turtles and coral conservation.

- Afternoon: Take a family bicycle ride to explore the island's lush landscapes.

- Evening: Dine at a family-friendly beachside restaurant.

*Day 6: Water Adventures**

- Morning: Go paddleboarding or kayaking with the family.

- Afternoon: Snorkel in the lagoon and introduce the kids to the underwater world.

- Evening: Celebrate your family adventure with a special dinner at the resort.

Day 7: Departure*

- Morning: Spend your last hours on the island enjoying the resort's amenities or the beach.

- Afternoon: Check out and transfer to Bora Bora Airport for your departure.

These sample itineraries offer a range of experiences, from adventure to romance and family-friendly activities, allowing you to tailor your trip to your interests and preferences.

Key Areas in Bora bora

Key areas in Bora Bora to help you get an idea of the island's layout:

1. **Vaitape**:

- Vaitape is the main town and the administrative center of Bora Bora. Here, you'll find the majority of the island's shops, banks, post offices, and government buildings. It's also where Bora Bora's main harbor is located.

2. **Matira Beach**:

- Matira Beach is one of Bora Bora's most famous beaches, known for its stunning white sands and crystal-clear waters. It's a popular spot for sunbathing and swimming.

3. **Mount Otemanu**:

- This is the highest peak on the island, rising to 2,385 feet (727 meters). It's a dormant volcano and a popular destination for hikers and nature enthusiasts.

4. **Mount Pahia**:

- Another notable peak on the island, Mount Pahia offers hiking opportunities and panoramic views.

5. **Motus**:

- Bora Bora is surrounded by small islets called motus. These islets often have beautiful beaches and are perfect for day trips, picnics, and water sports.

6. **Coral Gardens**:

- Located in the lagoon, Coral Gardens is a popular snorkeling spot with vibrant coral reefs and diverse marine life.

7. **Bora Bora Lagoonarium**:

- The Bora Bora Lagoonarium is a controlled environment where you can observe and interact with marine life, including sharks and rays.

8. **Bora Bora Airport**:

- The airport is situated on the motu of Motu Mute and provides the main gateway to Bora Bora. It's where most visitors arrive on the island.

9. **Resorts**:

- Bora Bora is famous for its luxurious overwater bungalows and high-end resorts. There are numerous resorts located on motus and around the island, each offering its own unique experience.

10. **Matira Point**:

- Matira Point is a scenic area where you can enjoy views of the lagoon, beaches, and lush vegetation. It's a popular spot for photography.

Whether you're looking for a romantic honeymoon, a family vacation, or a solo adventure, Bora Bora has something to offer every type of traveler.

Made in the USA
Las Vegas, NV
08 February 2024

85509796R00079